I Pursue After You

All Because You Are God:
A 21 Day Devotional

By

Jen'nea Sumo, PhD, RN

I Pursue After You

Cover design by Jasmine Powell
Email: admin@jesjazzy.com

Library of Congress Cataloging-in-Publication Data:
An application to register this book for cataloging has been
submitted to the Library of Congress.
ISBN: 978-0-692-13446-7

Contact

Email: info@allbecauseyouaregod.org

Acknowledgements

To my husband, you are a great man. I am so honored to be on this life journey with you and the children. Thank you for all of your support and encouragement.

To my mother-in-love, you were the first person to suggest that I should write a devotional. Thank you for always sowing love and wisdom in my life.

To my grandmother, Carol, you are truly the best granny in the world. I love you and am so thankful that you are mine.

To my mother, you are the most loving, kind person I know. In fact, you often take better care of others than you do for yourself. I pray that God blesses you abundantly for the genuine, compassionate care you give to others.

Table of Contents

Forward

This is a very exciting time to be a believer. We are witnessing God's Word through a move of the Holy Spirit manifesting Himself, releasing miracles and breakthroughs in the lives of His people. As we continue to humble ourselves and pray, believing that He is a rewarder of those who diligently seek Him (Hebrews 11:6), I believe we will see an even greater measure of the power of His Word demonstrated in the lives of believers. As we seek the face of God (His presence) I believe the hand of God (His blessings) will be extended even the more so.

In this devotional, Dr. Jen'nea Sumo shares insight through study, experience and revelation. This devotional truly is a tool that can be used to help build strong believers.

I have had the pleasure of knowing Dr. Sumo for many years. I have witnessed her stand on the promises of God. She is one that not only believes God, she has a bold unique, matter of fact way of trusting Him beyond measure (Philippians 4:13). Dr. Sumo is one who is passionate about her pursuit of purpose. This devotional is an extraordinary example of her desire to see others maximize their potential through pursuing God and spending quality time in prayer.

I highly recommend this devotional. As you implement the teachings, expect to be transformed from the inside out, walking out and living in a realm beyond what you have previously experienced.

Prophetess Delores Bell
Reformation Ministry

Prelude

I am blessed to be a part of a wonderful sisterhood called the Prayer Warriors. In 2017, some of my Prayer Warrior sisters and I attended the Women of Purpose Conference hosted by Evangelist Kemisha Lewis. This devotional was birthed because of the life changing experience I had while attending the conference.

While at the conference, I saw something I had never seen before. I saw Heaven on Earth. I remember looking up toward the front of the church and seeing all races of people on one accord and with one heart. I thought to myself, this looks like Heaven. When I turned and looked at Natalie, one of my prayer partners, she looked like an angel. I cannot fully explain what I experienced, but what I do know is that God gave me a glimpse of the unity and love He desires to be on Earth as it is in Heaven.

At the conference, Apostle Regina Martin was praying and ministering deliverance from Hadassah. Many of us know the Biblical story of Esther and how she helped to save the Jewish people. (If you are unfamiliar with the story read the Book of Esther.) We know her as the wife of a Persian king, but we do not know her by her original name, Hadassah.

Apostle Martin spoke about how Esther had to let go of "Hadassah" to bring in Esther. Hadassah was not raised in royalty. She did not have the training to be a queen (part of a royal family). Hadassah represented fear and history that could try to hold her back from fulfilling her destiny. Apostle Martin personally ministered to me that evening. She prayed for me and called out areas where Hadassah was operating in my life. I received a great deliverance that night and years of insecurity, lack of self-esteem and fear were broken off of me.

What I heard listening to Apostle Martin is that in order to walk into destiny, we must be willing to let go of feelings and behaviors that would cause us to believe that we are not God's children. The fact is when someone accepts Jesus as their Lord and Savior, they become a child of God (sonship). God's children must let go of feelings and beliefs that could delay them from receiving the full benefits that Jesus provided when He died on the Cross. With Jesus' sacrifice, we have access to the Kingdom of God.

After Apostle Martin ministered, she looked at me and said, "Go back and tell your pastors what transpired today". I obeyed her direction. I left the conference with a deeper understanding that Jesus is coming back for a people who understand their sonship and who are willing to walk it out. Walking out sonship involves allowing the Holy Spirit to lead, guide and direct to the fulfillment of purpose.

It may sound strange to some, but God does speak. In fact, He was talking to me while I was at the conference. I struggled with the Lord. I said to

God, "You keep telling me all these things you have for me to do, but I do not know how to do these things. I have not been fully trained. I do not even know where to start." The Holy Spirit said to me, "All I require of you is to be a yielded and obedient vessel and I will do the rest."

After attending the Women of Purpose Conference, I knew I had to share what God has shown me regarding pursuing His heart. I wrote this devotional because I choose to be a yielded and obedient vessel to my God. Let me be clear about the God I am talking about. I believe in the God of Abraham, Isaac and Jacob. This God is the God who Jesus prayed to. The God that Jesus said, "I only do what I see my father doing". There is only one true God and this God manifests Himself as three persons (God the Father, God the Son and God the Holy Spirit).

Introduction

I am what one would call an extroverted introvert. I can participate in social environments where someone may believe I am extroverted, but really, I am an introvert. I am private, quiet and thought filled. For years I have been a silent worshipper. A silent worshipper has a heart to pursue God but keeps to themselves. They do not always share what they see God is doing and requiring. I know now that I cannot be a silent worshipper. I know I must tell others about what God has shown me about pursuing His heart. So, let's begin.

One of the first things God showed me about pursuing His heart is that the pursuit requires humility. One must be humble and understand that he/she needs God and cannot make it without Him. The idea of "making it" may sound odd because there are many people walking around, who may not know God, but seem to be doing just fine. While others are walking around, who confess to know God, and seem to be struggling with life's trials. Yes, "making it" is about how we journey through life, but it is also about fulfillment of purpose.

When I say we cannot make it without Him, I am saying we cannot fulfill the purpose He has for our lives without Him. He is the creator. He is the one with the master plan. If we want to fulfill purpose, we must pursue Him. And when one pursues God regarding purpose, they must pursue from a position of love. They must desire to build relationship with God for He is a relational God.

" I am the vine, ye are the branches: He that abideth in me, and I in Him, the same bringeth forth much fruit: for without me ye can do nothing"(John 15:5).

God desires relationship and made us (mankind) for relationship with Him. He put in us purpose and destiny. He clearly has stated that we need to abide in Him and Him with us for that "much fruit" (Great Purpose) to be produced. God never intended for us to lack or to live a life that does not fulfill purpose, but instead He gave us the greatest gift of all (to help us produce "much fruit"). He gave us Himself, His Son and the Holy Spirit. He desires that we come to know Him. Through Him we find everything we need to fulfill our "Great Purpose". The journey toward doing great things for God starts with pursuing His heart and a relationship with Him.

King Hezekiah is an example of a man who pursued God's heart. The Bible says:

He trusted in the Lord God of Israel; so that after him was none like him among all the kings of Judah, nor any that were before him. For he clave to the Lord, and departed not from following him, but kept his commandments, which the Lord commanded Moses. And the Lord was with him; and he prospered whithersoever he went forth: and he rebelled against the king of Assyria, and served him not (2 Kings 18:5-7).

God's heart is connected to His directions. By following God's directions, King Hezekiah pursued God's heart. King Hezekiah "clave" to God. Clave is the past tense of the word cleave. In the Merriam-Webster dictionary cleave is defined as "adhering closely and unwaveringly". When King Hezekiah followed God's directions, he obeyed God's will.

While you read this devotional, be like King Hezekiah. Cleave to God and His Word. While you read, consider what it means to pursue the heart of God. Think about what your pursuit means for you, your family, your community, and even the nations.

This devotional is a bit different from other devotionals. In it I provide food for thought regarding pursuing God's heart, but a lot of the next 21 days is about you following the guide provided, searching the scriptures and inquiring of God on your own. You will need to locate a concordance or use the internet to help you identify relevant scriptures for specific topics. In addition to studying and meditating on scriptures in the Bible (Word of God), you will be praying. You will be presented with opportunities to pray about what is on the heart of God. If you have never said a prayer or written out a prayer that is ok, now is the perfect time to start. Fear not, for God will direct your pen and your path. For those of you who are seasoned prayer warriors, get ready for God to expand your prayer life as you study to show yourselves approved and pray through these 21 days.

Directions

This devotional has 7 sections with 3 days in each section. You can complete the devotional in three ways: 1) Read the section narrative, the first day in the section and complete the thought exercise. Then read the remaining days in the section without revisiting the section narrative. 2) You may choose to review the section narrative, each day before you delve into the thought exercise for the day. 3) Or you may decide that you need more than 21 days to complete this journey and go through the devotional as God leads you.

You may read this devotional by yourself, with a friend, family member, or in a group. How you decide to take this journey is up to you. The only requirement is that you move through the devotional with great expectation. Begin and end this journey with great expectation from God, the One who desires your pursuit.

*Within this devotional, you will notice that when I speak of God, I capitalize words that are not normally capitalized. For instance, capitalizing the "he" when I speak of God is just my little way of honoring God within these typed pages.

Section 1: Why Pursue God's Heart?

When we pursue God's heart, we get to know his character and desires. We learn that He has good plans for his children and that He desires to bless us.

For the eyes of the Lord run to and fro throughout the whole Earth, to shew himself strong on the behalf of them whose heart is perfect toward him (2 Chronicles 16:9).

We learn that His thoughts and ways are higher than our own and that He greatly loves us. When we pursue God's heart, we understand that He is the "great" judge, holy, and requires a reverential fear. Reverential fear is not about being afraid of God, but about reverencing, honoring, and understanding who God is. It is about honoring and respecting God's authority. Most of all, we learn that pursuing the heart of God pleases Him. **Yes, God has a heart that can be pursued, and it is possible to please Him.**

So, although God is not human, he does have emotions. He can become angry, vexed and disappointed, but He can also be pleased. King David is an example of a man who pleased and pursued after God. King David was a worshipper. He reverenced God. He was one who sought God and took precautions to not offend God or anyone God considered anointed. King David's pursuit of God was so great that God called him a

9

man after His own heart (Acts 13:22). So yes, God has a heart that we can pursue.

We were made in God's image and just like we have emotions He has emotions. He gets angry. God the Father got angry with the Israelites because they took their eyes off of pursuing Him and sought after a golden calf to worship.

God said now then let Me alone, that My anger may burn against them and that I may destroy them; and I will make of you a great nation." Then Moses entreated the LORD his God, and said, "O LORD, why does Your anger burn against Your people whom You have brought out from the land of Egypt with great power and with a mighty hand? (Exodus 10:12)

Recently, God showed me He even has the emotion of sadness. One would not think that the God of the universe could be sad, but He gets sad when we (heirs of salvation) do not know Him and operate below our abilities. One day, I was driving into work, and God gave me an example of His compassionate heart for His people.

I pulled into a parking space, and when I looked behind me, I saw a woman who was pulling in directly behind me. She pulled up behind me almost as though she was about to hit my car. She stopped re-adjusted her car and parked right next to me on my right-hand side. I thought to myself, "Wow, she almost hit me, that is odd". But then I went on doing what I was doing. A few moments later, I looked up in her direction and the Holy Spirit said to me, "Pray for her she is worried". At that moment, I began to pray for the concern God showed me she was having.

I prayed a genuine prayer and asked God to send the deliverance and confidence she needed to overcome. After I prayed, I went on listening to praise and worship music and getting ready for work. When I was finally ready to get out of the car, I looked, and the woman was getting out of her car too. I thought to myself, "Now, that is strange, I have been sitting here for a while and she is getting out at the same time I am". Then the Holy Spirit spoke to me and said, "I want you to go tell her that I love her". I walked up a little bit to catch her and said, "good morning". She replied, "good morning" (as anyone would). When I proceeded to tell her what God wanted me to tell her [that He loves her and desires great things for her], she sheepishly said thank you and walked quickly to the elevator.

I was so glad I was obedient because I know how God works. Sometimes he allows us to sow the seed, then he sends someone else to water it, but he always gives the increase. I was glad I was obedient to be either the seed sower or the one who was watering the seed.

However, I am not sure how glad she was that I spoke to her. She looked very uncomfortable. The woman and I were the only people near the elevator. She entered the elevator and faced the wall with her left shoulder toward the elevator door. I thought to myself, "why is she standing so close to the wall". When the elevator doors opened, she hurried off the elevator.

As I stepped out of the elevator, the Holy Spirit said to me, "See my children do not know that I love them". He allowed me to feel some of the disappointment and sadness He feels because His children do not understand the love that He has for them. They do not have a full understanding that He desires to give His children the Kingdom.

I was so moved by His emotions that in the evening when my prayer warrior sisters got on our prayer call, I could not help but to tell them what happened with the woman on the elevator. I told them about how saddened our Abba Father is that His children do not fully understand how much He cares for them. As I talked to my sisters, I got so emotionally charged. I said, "What do I have to do to help His children understand that they are loved? I never want my God to feel saddened. He is such a great God who has given us everything". On that day, I became focused on doing what I can to help God's children understand their value to Him.

How often have we heard the scripture John 3:16? We hear about how God so loved the world that He gave His only begotten son. This scripture is not a scripture to take lightly. It is not one to gloss over, but it is a scripture to hold in our hearts. **God**

so loved. He loves us. And love is an emotion. And God's love is backed by action. He so loved that He gave us Jesus! Jesus so loved that He declared the coming of the Holy Spirit. The Holy Spirit (our comforter and guide) so loved that he lives inside us. The Bible says:

If you do not know love you do not know God. For God is Love— (1 John 4:8).

This lack of knowing His love is why God was so sad. His child did not know that He loved her, so she did not truly know Him!

Prayer

In Jesus name, I pray let it be this day that me and all those you desire for yourself (the heirs of salvation everywhere) come into the knowledge of You. For you are, a loving father, savior and guide. Help me Lord to know You and please You. Forgive me for any area of doubt, unbelief, disobedience, unforgiveness and any other iniquity that would try to keep me from knowing that You love me. Lord I believe that you have given me all I require for life and godliness. Let me not grieve You by doubting your love for me. Instead, teach me even more about You and Your love. Give me the grace I need to live a life that is pleasing to You. Let me and the heirs of salvation everywhere walk in full sonship. For Your Word says that the Earth yearns for the manifestation of the sons of God (*Romans 8:17-19*).

And I long for Your will to be done on Earth as it is in Heaven. In Jesus name I pray. Amen.

Day 1

Thought Exercise: King David was a man after God's own heart. What was it about King David that pleased God? What can you do in your own personal life to please God where God would call you a person after His heart?

Talk to God today. Ask Him how you can please Him. Then open your Bible and find scriptures that describe what pleases God. Take notes on what you uncover in your study today. Then write a prayer asking God for the grace to put forth action to do what pleases Him. Let God know that you desire to be a person after His heart.

And when he had removed him, he raised up unto them David to be their king; to whom also he gave testimony, and said, I have found David the son of Jesse, a man after mine own heart, which shall fulfil all my will (Acts 13:22).

Day 2

Thought Exercise: Studying the character of God the Father, God the Son and God the Holy Spirit helps us to understand the heart of God. What does Jesus mean when He says He is the way, the truth and the life? What can you learn about His heart from knowing that He is the way, truth, and life? Take notes from your study today and then write out a prayer asking Jesus to know Him more fully.

Jesus said to him "I am the way, the truth, and the life. No one comes to the Father except through me" (John 14:16 NKJV).

Day 3

Thought Exercise: God wants us to know Him as love. He wants us to know that we are loved. The Holy Spirit is given to us and shares with us the love of God.

Now hope does not disappoint, because the love of God has been poured out in our hearts by the Holy Spirit who was given to us (Romans 5:5 NKJV).

In fact, one fruit of the Holy Spirit is love.

But the fruit of the Spirit is love, joy, peace, longsuffering, gentleness, goodness, faith, meekness, temperance: against such there is no law (Galatians 5:22-23).

Use a concordance or search the internet for scriptures about love. Read those scriptures, take notes and meditate on the Word you uncover. Then write out a prayer regarding God's love based on what you find in the scriptures.

Section 2: What Does it Mean to Pursue God's Heart?

What does it mean to pursue after God's heart? Pursuing God's heart is about seeking after God and His Kingdom. As we pursue Him, we come to the place where His heart desires become our desires.

The first step to pursuing the heart of God is accepting that God is represented in three persons: God the Father, God the Son and God the Holy Spirit. Some people struggle with the thought that God is represented within this Holy Trinity. I personally like how Pastor Robert Morris (Gateway Church) explains the Trinity. He teaches that people will be better able to believe in the persons of God, once they understand that each person within the Trinity (Father, Son and Holy Spirit) is a function of a singular God. Therefore, God the Father has a different function than God the Son and God the Holy Spirit, but all functions operate from one God.

If someone accepts God the Father but rejects God the Son (Jesus), they are missing the characteristics of God's heart that Jesus possesses. Another person may seek after God the Father and God the Son but does not believe in God the Holy Spirit. This person's pursuit of God would be limited because they would not seek to understand the heart of God the Holy Spirit. Ultimately, to pursue God's heart one must focus on understanding the Trinity:

God the Father, God the Son and God the Holy Spirit!

Once there is attention given to the persons of the Trinity, the next step in pursuing God's heart is to enact the Ask, Seek, Knock principle. God never intended for us to walk around void of knowledge and understanding. In fact, He said in the Word:

If any of you lacks wisdom, let him ask of God, who gives to all liberally and without reproach, and it will be given to him (James 1:5; NKJV).

Jesus said: *"Ask and it will be given to you; seek and you will find; knock and the door will be opened to you. For everyone who asks receives; the one who seeks finds; and to the one who knocks, the door will be opened (Matthew 7:7-8).*

Ask God to reveal His heart to you. Seek Him in the Bible and through prayer. Knock means that when you ask and seek, and God gives direction, you obey his guidance and put forth action regarding what He tells you to do. Because He is a God of love, He will direct you to move in love. The knock is like love in motion. It is a movement of obedience.

Obadiah is a great example of the Knock. He had a reverential fear of God. He did what he knew was on God's heart. In a time of distress for God's prophets, Obadiah took 100 prophets and hid them by fifty in two caves (1 Kings 18: 3-4).

The final step of pursuing God's heart is all about laboring to please God ("Laboring" to please God the Father, God the Son and God the Holy Spirit). When most people hear the word labor they may think about toiling or hard work. But when you labor to seek and please God, you do so not by your strength but by His strength. In fact, when you pursue after God you find rest for your soul. Jesus said:

All things have been delivered to Me by My Father, and no one knows the Son except the Father. Nor does anyone know the Father except the Son, and the one to whom the Son wills to reveal Him. Come to Me, all you who labor and are heavy laden, and I will give you rest. Take My yoke upon you and learn from Me, for I am gentle and lowly in heart, and you will find rest for your souls. For My yoke is easy and My burden is light (Matthew 11: 27-30 NKJV).

Just as God never intended for us to be without knowledge and understanding, He never wanted us to struggle. He has given us a way of escape from the "labor" that involves toiling. We must believe, pursue, and endeavor to please God. Then He gives the grace to labor to enter His rest. The Bible says:

There remaineth therefore a rest to the people of God. For he that is entered into his rest, he also hath ceased from his own works, as God did from his (Hebrews 4: 9-10).

Laboring to enter God's rest requires trust and self-evaluation. You must examine your heart-and be willing to surrender your heart to Him. To say to God, "You are my God, I am your child. I look to you. For you are my help and my hope (Psalm 39:7). Father your ways are higher than my ways and your thoughts are higher than my thoughts (Isaiah 55:9)! Show me your ways, show me your thoughts. Create in me a clean heart and renew a right spirit within me (Psalm 51:10)".

It is true, we may not be perfect when we pursue God's heart or perfect as we labor to enter His rest. However, when we pursue God, we are positioning ourselves to understand what is on the heart of God and then we can put forth action to please Him. **We must remember that God desires yielded obedient vessels and promises to do the rest.**

Prayer

In Jesus name, I proclaim, Lord you are great in all the Earth. Give me and the heirs of salvation everywhere the desire to know You for who You are. Give us grace to seek You through Your Word and through prayer. Allow us to know You as the God of

Abraham, Isaac, and Jacob. Lord I pray that this journey of pursuing You will help me know You as my God. While I journey through this devotional, give me wisdom to understand Your ways and Your thoughts. Share more with me Lord about the Trinity (God the Father, God the Son, and God the Holy Spirit). For I know that there is strength in the Trinity. Your Word says that a three-cord strand is not easily broken (Ecclesiastes 4:12). There is much that You desire for me to understand about the Trinity and I am open to receive the revelation You desire to give. Share Your heart with me, oh Lord, and give me a tender heart to not only receive instruction, but to obey Your direction. In Jesus name I pray. Amen.

Day 4

Thought Exercise: Pursuing God's heart is about learning who He is. Understanding the names of God is a great way to learn about God. Within the Bible, God the Father is known by many names (e.g., Yahweh, Jehovah Jireh, Jehovah Nissi, Elohim, El Shaddai, and I Am That I Am).

Take some time today to look up names of God the Father. What does His names say about His character? For example, what does the name Jehovah Nissi (Exodus 5:5) say about God's character? Study the various names of God the Father and write a prayer asking to be shown His character in His Word and in your life.

Day 5

Thought Exercise: Just as God the Father has many names, Jesus (God the Son), also has many names. Jesus is called the Messiah, Yeshua, Lamb of God, Lion of Judah ...etc. Take time today to look through scripture and study the various names of Jesus. Read *Matthew 1:23* and ask God to increase your understanding of Jesus being Emmanuel (God with us). Read *Revelations 5:2-5*. What do you learn about Jesus' character from knowing that He is the Lion of Judah? Take notes and write out a prayer based on what you review about Jesus' names. Your prayer may be to gain a deeper revelation about the names you reviewed.

Day 6

Thought Exercise: God the Holy Spirit also has many names. He is the Spirit of Truth (*John 14:17*); Spirit of Faith (*2 Corinthians 4:13*); Spirit of the Lord God (*Isaiah 61:1*); Spirit of Holiness (*Roman 1:4*); Teacher (*1 Corinthians 2:13*); Comforter (*John 16:7*); Spirit of Revelation (*Ephesians 1:17*); Spirit of Counsel (*Isaiah 11:2*). Select at least three of the above scriptures, study the scriptures, take notes and write out a prayer regarding the scriptures you reviewed today.

Section 3: Levels of Pursuing God's Heart

In the Bible, the books *II Chronicles* and *II Kings* have numerous examples of kings and their pursuit of God. From reading these books, God showed me that there are levels of being in pursuit of His heart. The first level is a stagnant level (*not pursuing what is right in his sight and not having a perfect heart*). In this first level, there may or may not be a knowledge of God. There is no demonstrated reverence for God. I am not saying that people who are at level 1 are not Christians. In fact, many Christians have confessed Jesus as their Lord and Savior, they are just not in pursuit of Him. Basically, they are not asking. They are not seeking. They are not knocking and because they have no pursuit of God, they have no change in heart. Yes, level of pursuit is connected to the heart. I believe level of pursuit and matters of the heart are interwoven whereby one strengthens the other. Pursuing after God changes the heart of man, and when man has a change in heart, man pursues after God.

The second level of pursuit is a level of partial pursuit. *Where a believer does what is right in the sight of God but not with a perfect heart.* In *II Chronicles 25:2* we see an excellent example of level 2.

26

And he (King Joash) did that which was right in the sight of the LORD, but not with a perfect heart (2 Chronicles 25:2).

Joash was a King in Jerusalem. He did what was right in the sight of the Lord as long as Jehoiada the priest was living. However, when Jehoiada died Joash listened to the princes of Judah and no longer followed God. God sent more than one prophet to King Joash, but He would not listen. The situation got so bad for Joash that he killed Zechariah (Jehoiada's son) (*II Chronicles 24:22-23*). The Bible says that King Joash did not remember the kindness of Jehoiada.

King Joash did well to obey God when Jehoiada was living and helping to guide him. One could say, King Joash did what was right and listened to wise counsel so why is his heart not perfect? King Joash would have demonstrated a perfect heart if he would have continued to follow God when Jehoiada (the priest) died. Doing God's will was not fully engrained in King Joash's heart. If doing God's will was the focus of King Joash's heart, when Jehoiada died he would have sought God instead of listening to the princes of Judah (read this occurrence in full detail in *II Chronicles, chapter 24*).

The third and final level of pursuing God's heart is the level of *Full Pursuit*. In this level, one *does what is right in the eyes of God and has a perfect heart before God*. In *Isaiah 38*, King Hezekiah demonstrates the level of Full Pursuit. It was his Full Pursuit which gave him the boldness to pray for healing and it was his Full Pursuit which turned God's heart and allowed King Hezekiah to live 15 more years.

In those days was Hezekiah sick unto death. And Isaiah the prophet the son of Amoz came unto him, and said unto him, Thus saith the LORD, Set thine house in order: for thou shalt die, and not live. Then Hezekiah turned his face toward the wall, and prayed unto the LORD, And said, Remember now, O LORD, I beseech thee, how **_I have walked before thee in truth and with a perfect heart, and have done that which is good in thy sight._** *And Hezekiah wept sore. Then came the Word of the LORD to Isaiah, saying, Go, and say to Hezekiah, Thus saith the LORD, the God of David thy father, I have heard thy prayer, I have seen thy tears: behold, I will add unto thy days fifteen years. And I will deliver thee and this city out of the hand of the king of Assyria: and I will defend this city. And this shall be a sign unto thee from the LORD, that the LORD will do this thing that he hath spoken; Behold, I will bring again the shadow of the degrees, which is gone down in the sun dial of Ahaz, ten degrees backward. So the sun returned ten degrees, by which degrees it was gone down (Isaiah 38).*

King Hezekiah had a reverential fear of God, so his motives were not to pursue God to get something from Him. King Hezekiah's pursuit of God lead him to come boldly before the Lord and bring back to God's remembrance that he had walked in truth, with a perfect heart and did what pleased God. Imagine if King Hezekiah could not say that he walked in truth or had a perfect heart or did what pleased God. King Hezekiah may not have had the same boldness in his prayer. He may not have had the same unction to pray because he may have thought that he deserved the sickness.

I am not saying that God does not heal those who do not fully pursue Him. God is a healer and brings forth healing by the stripes of Jesus. And that healing is for all those that call on the name of Jesus. What I am saying is that doing what is right in the sight of God and continually working on perfecting your heart is pleasing to God. So much so that God answers the prayers of those who pursue Him. Having a perfect heart does not mean being perfect. It means seeking the one who is perfect and being in a continual place of repentance. For God surely honors a tender and humble heart.

In *II Kings*, the Word of God demonstrates His acceptance of those whose heart is tender and humble before him. When King Josiah heard the Word of the Lord (*II Kings 22:10-13*), he sent his men to inquire of Huldah (a prophetess in Jerusalem). Huldah released a Word from God. The Word described what God planned to do because the people had forsaken Him and went after other gods.

Because King Josiah's heart was tender toward God and he sought out the Lord, the prophetess proclaimed:

> *"Because thine heart was tender, and thou hast humbled thyself before the Lord, when thou heardst what I spake against this place and against the inhabitants thereof, that they should become a desolation and a curse, and hast rent thy clothes, and wept before me; I also have heard thee, saith the Lord. God said: Behold therefore, I will gather thee unto thy fathers, and thou shalt be gathered into thy grave in peace: and thine eyes shall not see all the evil which I will bring upon this place"* (*II Kings 22:19-20*).

King Josiah demonstrated a level of Full Pursuit. When he knew the will of God, his heart was tender towards the things of God. His Full Pursuit kept him safe in a time where God had decided to release His wrath upon the land. We are living in a time where we cannot be moved by what others think or say about us. Nor can we be judgmental and fault finding for what we see other people doing. Just as other people must come to God for themselves, we must walk in love and come to God for ourselves. We must endeavor to live a life in Full Pursuit of God. It is in the Full Pursuit where we come to know Him and where we have an opportunity to receive His supernatural protection.

What if King Josiah had not rent his clothes and wept before God? What if he did not decide to pursue God? Well, he would have not had the covering that God provided Him. King Josiah went to his grave in peace and did not see God's wrath. Because King Josiah did not experience the wrath, those among him also did not experience the wrath. This story helped me to see that our level of pursuit can have a great impact on those around us. Full Pursuit is the highest level and the level that God desires His children to operate within.

Prayer

In Jesus name, Lord I desire to be a believer who is operating and living out of the level of Full Pursuit. I desire to seek You while it is day. I desire to learn of You and have a heart transformation where Your desires become my desires, and your will is my will. Forgive me for any area of delay regarding my pursuit of You. If it has been a delay in me doing what is right in Your eyes, forgive me. I repent. If it has been a delay of me having a pure heart before You, forgive me. I repent. Lord remove all barriers that would attempt to hinder my pursuit of You and Your Kingdom. For I know that Your Word says:

Seek ye first the kingdom of God and His righteousness and all these things will be added unto You (Matthew 6:33).

I desire to be obedient to this Word not because of the things added, but because of the relationship that will grow between You and I as I pursue after You. Lord allow my pursuit to make a lasting positive difference in the lives of those in my sphere of influence. I bless You Lord and love you. In Jesus name I pray. Amen.

Day 7

Thought Exercise: The Bible says that someone can pray amiss and not receive answers to their prayers. Read James 4:3 to review reasons why prayers may not be answered. Then identify scriptures that demonstrate answered prayers.

What was the position of the heart of the person who received the answered prayer? What were their motives? Search the scriptures, take notes, and write a prayer based on what you reviewed today. (The story of Hannah (*1 Samuel*) is a very good example of someone who received an answered prayer.)

Day 8

Thought Exercise: Jesus is our big Brother. He is our example! Today search the scriptures and locate three scriptures that identify the position of Jesus' heart toward God the Father. Write out a prayer and ask God to position your heart as Jesus' heart is positioned to serve and please God the Father.

Day 9

Thought Exercise: Write out a prayer to God concerning the levels of pursuing His heart. Ask Him to get and/or stay on the level of Full Pursuit. Take the time to talk to Him about the things that have hindered your pursuit. Then spend some time in prayer and listen to what God has to share with you. Prayer is a conversation. We talk to God, but He talks back to us. Today, take time to tarry in His presence to hear what He has to say.

Section 4: How to Pursue the Heart of God?

Pursuing the heart of God is connected to knowing His will and doing His will. The way to know the will of God is to spend time with Him. You must be open to listening to His plans and desires and what it is He wants to do through you. Knowing the will of God also involves seeking God. King David is a perfect example of one who pursued after God's heart. In fact, God called him "a man after my own heart" (Acts 13:22). King David trusted God. He knew that God is the source of accurate information and guidance which is why he was careful to inquire of God before he made important decisions. When David was anointed King of Israel, He inquired of the Lord to gain insight on what to do concerning the Philistines.

And David enquired of the LORD, saying, Shall I go up to the Philistines? Wilt thou deliver them into mine hand? And the LORD said unto David, Go up: for I will doubtless deliver the Philistines into thine hand (2 Samuel 5:19).

It was David's obedience to inquire of God that gave him directed action and victory. In fact, it is recorded that God did not always say yes to David's question whether he should go up against his enemies (1 Chronicles 14:13-16). In this passage, God said no, but gave him specific direction that caused him to still be victorious.

Then the Philistines once again made a raid on the valley. Therefore, David inquired again of God, and God said to him, "You shall not go up after them; circle around them and come upon them in front of the mulberry trees. And it shall be, when you hear a sound of marching in the tops of the mulberry trees, then you shall go out to battle, for God has gone out before you to strike the camp of the Philistines." So David did as God commanded him, and they drove back the army of the Philistines from Gibeon as far as Gezer (1 Chronicles 14:13-17 NKJV).

King David trusted God's counsel and took the time to gain His counsel before he made decisions. King David was also a man after God's own heart because he feared God. King David had a reverential fear of God. Reverential fear means that he knew that God is holy and powerful. He reverenced God's authority. King Saul not only threatened David's life; he was in hot pursuit of David to kill him. David's reverence for God was evident. Even after David was given opportunity to kill King Saul, he did not kill him. Because God once anointed Saul and appointed him as King, David refused to harm God's anointed. God had given David the kingdom, but Saul was still king. This reverential fear may have been the basis of King David's worship of God. He had to worship. He loved God. Even when his own wife made negative comments regarding how he worshipped God in the presence of others. King David said to Michal (his wife):

> *"It was before the LORD, who chose me rather than your father or anyone from his house when he appointed me ruler over the LORD's people Israel—I will celebrate before the LORD. I will become even more undignified than this, and I will be humiliated in my own eyes" (2 Samuel 6:21-22).*

So, what does it look like to pursue the heart of God? King David pursued God's heart by seeking, trusting, staying in a place of reverential fear and worshipping God. King David was obedient to the will of God which could be the reason God called him a man after His own heart. Knowing God's will is like knowing Him. There is an intimacy between God and man when man knows His will and obeys. As you spend time with God, He speaks to you. Knowing His will becomes easier because you know his character and when you know His character, you know the things that please him.

For me knowing God's will has come from reading His Word, knowing His character and revelation from the Holy Spirit. Sometimes that revelation comes directly to me from God and sometimes He uses his children to speak prophetic Words that bring forth revelation and direction.

When I was preparing to graduate from nursing school, I was very distraught. I was concerned because I did not know the next steps to

38

take. I had been praying and asking God for direction, but I felt like He was not moving quick enough. I felt like He was not hearing my prayers. I had begun asking God, "Do you even hear me when I pray to you". One Wednesday evening, I went to Apostle Darryl O'Neil's church (Crusaders Church West). Apostle O'Neil had on many occasions talked about a prophetic husband and wife team who had previously ministered at the church. He spoke of them before, but I had never had the opportunity to partake in their ministry. Well, this particular Wednesday night, I came to Bible study thinking Apostle would be teaching, but instead the husband and wife team were there.

I sat in the far back and listened as they ministered. I sat there thinking to myself. "Oh Lord, I need a Word from You". Even though my heart was crying out, I was physically hiding behind the person sitting in front of me. I was hiding because I did not want to look needy. So even though I was sitting in my chair pleading with God to use his children to give me a Word from Him, I was slouching down behind the person in front of me. When the husband was prophesying the wife was praying and when the wife was prophesying the husband was praying. As they were ministering, I was participating in prayer. I was praying with and for everyone who was receiving Words from God.

But I also was sitting in my seat asking God for a Word. For some reason I said, "God I want a

Word, but not from the husband, I want a Word from the wife". Toward the end of the service, it was getting late and I could tell the service was wrapping up. I was still hiding and praying when I heard the wife say, "the young woman in the black sweater". She was speaking toward my direction. I looked around me and behind me and she said- "yes you". I stood up and this is what she said:

"I looked back at you and heard God say- your heart is crying out. God says: I hear you. I heard you yesterday, I heard you the day before. But I am bringing you to a new place says God. There are some things I want you to embrace and as you begin to embrace them, I will begin to do those things that I promised you (says the spirit of God). Two new jobs, I just saw two new jobs are going to come your way. Two new jobs, and God says tell you don't go after the one that is paying the highest money because that is short term. Go after the one that is paying the lower money for the long-term situation that will take care of you. I hear God saying that within this new job, the long term; you will be getting the training in terms of schooling that you didn't get. God says you will get it through this job. He also said tell you- In the last part of May and the first 2 weeks in June- things will speed up for you. So even though this season has been like rough and tough God says I am turning it all around for you because I love you and because You love me".

What is so amazing about that prophetic Word is that for 1- my heart was truly crying out, 2- God answered my question as to whether He heard me when I prayed to him, and 3- exactly what she prophesized came to pass. I was offered 2 new jobs. And one of those jobs turned out to be school. I chose to go to school when I was offered an opportunity to earn my doctorate. School was the job paying the least. I, like King David, pursued God's heart. I pursued His will and he sent His daughter to help direct me to the next phase in my life.

Prayer

In Jesus name, I come before you today asking for grace. Father even as you share in your Word that King David asked you for the grace to know your will. He said:

"Teach me to do thy will; for thou art my God: thy spirit is good; lead me into the land of the uprightness (Psalms 143:10).

Father, I pray for that same grace. I desire to know You and what pleases You. I not only want to know what pleases You, God I want to do what pleases You. Share Your heart with me Lord and give me grace to be obedient to Your direction. Put me in the right place at the right time with the right people. As You send people my way to minister to me and allow me to stay on the path You have for me, Lord also send me to people You have for me to encourage and be a vessel to help guide them on the path you have for them. Lord have your way in the lives of Your children and all those You desire for yourself. In Jesus name I pray. Amen.

Day 10

Thought Exercise: Apostle Paul talks about the importance of the knowledge of God's will in the life of a believer.

For this cause we also since the day we heard it, do not cease to pray for you and to desire that ye might be filled with the knowledge of His will in all wisdom and spiritual understanding. That ye might walk worthy of the Lord unto all pleasing, being fruitful in every good work, and increasing in the knowledge of God (Colossians 9-10).

Today study the Biblical story of Noah. He knew and did the will of God. Take notes on what you learn about Noah's character and write a prayer based on what you review today.

Day 11

Thought Exercise: Jesus is the ultimate example of knowing and doing the will of God. In the Bible, He sought God early. He had a continual relationship and communion with God. He is clear. He only does what He sees His Father do.

What do you see God the Father doing? Today, look for scriptures regarding God's will. Take notes on what you review. Then pray and ask God to show you what He is doing and how you can support His agenda.

Day 12

Thought Exercise: Jesus told those that tarried, to wait for the comforter (Holy Spirit) (*Acts 1-14*). It was through obedience that they received the activation to press into the next level. They waited and when the Holy Spirit came upon them, they received power. Jesus knew the will of God the Father when He told them to tarry. He knew the Holy Spirit was coming.

Today, pray to understand the will of the father and to obey. Read the outcome of being obedient in *Acts 2:1-13*. Take notes on what happened when the Holy Spirit came. And pray and ask God for a deeper revelation of His will. Thank Him for giving you a heart of flesh that is obedient. Ask God to soften the hearts of His children that they will be obedient and pursue after Him. Pray for your community that those who know God will come to know Him more fully and those who do not know Him will have an encounter with Him.

Section 5: Barriers to Pursuing God's Heart

There are numerous barriers to pursuing God's heart. All barriers start first in the heart. Unforgiveness, faithlessness, and disobedience are examples of barriers. These barriers are conditions of the heart that go against the Word of God. God clearly instructs us to forgive others (Matthew 6:14), requires that His children operate in faith (Hebrews 11:6) and desires for the heirs of salvation to obey His teaching (John 14:23).

Unforgiveness is like a deceiving friendship. One holds on to unforgiveness (their friend) almost as a safety mechanism to protect themselves from future attacks from others. Unforgiveness is a self-centered condition of the heart. Unforgiveness would tell someone that they are more important than someone else. That they have a right to not forgive because of what someone else did to them (some offense that wounded them).

When our spouse, sibling, friend, neighbor, co-worker or even someone we do not know well brings offense, the root of unforgiveness begins to form to prevent relationships, connection and love from operating. Anyone who is holding unforgiveness may feel that they are "in the right" and it is the other person who is "in the wrong". But the truth is that holding unforgiveness in the heart is not aligned with God's plan for His church.

And be kind to one another,
tenderhearted, forgiving one another, even as God in
Christ forgave you (Ephesians 4:32 NKJV).

Faithlessness is a heart condition that is a great barrier to pursuing God's heart. It is connected to purpose and destiny. Faith is so important to God that He clearly tells us that faith is a requirement to please Him (*Hebrews 11:6*). If we do not have faith in God, then it is like we are telling God, we do not believe that He holds our purpose and destiny. It is as if we are letting God know that we do not believe that He can bring to pass the plan He has for us.

With faith in God we can travel through life with confidence that the work He began in us he is faithful to complete it. He (the creator) knows what the plan is for each of His children. In order to learn the plan, we <u>must</u> pursue Him.

Like unforgiveness and faithlessness, disobedience is outside of God's will. In fact, being disobedient to God's direction is like one pursuing their self-will and fulfilling the needs of one's heart instead of pursuing God's heart. We can knowingly or unknowingly be disobedient. God says that His people perish for lack of knowledge (*Hosea 4:6*). Could it be that the perishing is connected to disobedience? If we are not reading the Word of God and acting on the Word of God, then we may perish because of being ignorant of necessary information God wants to share with us. This example of

47

disobedience is connected to being ignorant regarding the Word of God.

A good illustration of known and unknown disobedience is found when we think about tithing. God says:

Bring ye all the tithes into the storehouse, that there may be meat in mine house, and prove me now herewith, saith the LORD of hosts, if I will not open you the windows of Heaven, and pour you out a blessing, that there shall not be room enough to receive it (Malachi 3:10).

Now there are two ways to be disobedient when it comes to tithing. Person A is disobedient because they choose to not tithe even though they know that the Word of God instructs them to tithe. Person B is disobedient even though they have not read the Word and have never been taught to tithe. Person B is not practicing willful disobedience when it comes to tithing but they are still being disobedient to the Word because they do not know the Word.

Now, I know there has been much controversy and debate when it comes to tithing. Some say that tithing is an old testament requirement and is no longer needed under the new testament. I am not here to debate whether one should tithe or not tithe. I am simply here to say that giving to God should not be a struggle. Giving to the church that feeds your spirit and soul should not be a challenge. When we give to God, we are not giving something that He has not already first given us.

I wonder how many more people would give tithe if God asked for 5% instead of 10%. Or stop tithing if He asked for 25% instead of 10%. Tithing is clearly a heart issue. Some say God does not need our money. This statement is true, but God does desire our hearts and if our heart and expectation is rooted in how much money we have, how much money we need, or how much money we can save then we are missing the big picture.

God knows that His children have needs. He knows all about our bills and responsibilities and even our desires. The truth is God desires our hearts. Tithing and giving to the Kingdom of God is a way to tell God, I love you. I trust, you and I honor you.

If you or someone you know is on the fence or completely against tithing, I encourage you and them to do what God says and try Him. See if He does not pour you out a blessing you do not have room to receive (Malachi 3:8-10). I encourage you to ask God to show you the motives of your heart and if there be any hidden fear. Ask God to show you any area in your life where you are continuing to lead and have not surrendered to Him. Then pray that he delivers you from all fear, doubt, and unbelief when it comes to giving to Him. Ask God to show you His plan concerning the tithe and giving. So yes, not tithing can be a barrier to pursuing God's heart not because God needs your money but because he desires your heart.

Plus, I believe that willingness to give unto God helps him measure how much he can give you. If he can trust you with a little, then He can trust you with much. He knows that if you are willing to give in love and with a cheerful heart than when he gives you abundance, He can trust you to be obedient if He tells you to give away what He has given you. The Bible says where your treasure is your heart will be also, and if your treasure is in your money, then that is where your heart resides. God wants your heart. He wants His children to have a willing obedient heart.

This conversation about barriers to pursuing God's heart is not intended to bring forth condemnation. In fact, the real purpose of this dialogue is to help you be cognizant of barriers that may try to hinder your pursuit of God. The truth is all have sinned and fallen short of the glory of God (*Romans 3:23*). It does not matter if we have tried to live sinless lives, our attempt to be sinless and live righteous is still like filthy rags to a Holy God (*Isaiah 64:6*). The amazing thing is that even though we may make mistakes and think, behave, or respond in ways that are displeasing to God. God wants us to know that we have not missed it, if we have breath in our bodies, we have an opportunity to get up and start over.

I know I have felt as though I have missed it on numerous occasions. For example, for me, entertaining distractions is a barrier to pursuing God's heart. I am very analytical. I enjoy watching programs that have mysteries and suspense where you must work to figure out what is going on. I like watching programs that can provide a sense of surprise when something happens that was unexpected. Well, a few years ago when I was journaling the Holy Spirit told me to stay away from things that bring distraction to me. He was telling me to stay on course because tv is something that is a time stealer for me. I can get really caught up in the thinking behind tv and when a tv show has episodes that come on over and over and over my day could be wasted. I am stuck watching tv trying to see what happens next.

Although, I know about the importance of me avoiding distractions, I also sometimes like to decompress by watching tv. Recently I became distracted with a tv program. When I finally broke away from the program, I was so disappointed that I wasted time watching tv for so long. Thirty minutes would have been fine, but three hours when I have other things to do, was way too much. I came to my prayer room and repented to God. I said God forgive me for wasting that time, I told God that the reason I like watching the program is because of the thinking that goes on and the mysteries.

I prayed and spent time with Him. During the time I was spending with him, I think I fell asleep. I say think, because I could not tell if I was dreaming or if I was awake, but I saw a name flash across my closed eyes. When I woke up (or came to) I began to pray. I did not know what the certain name meant so I prayed that if it was a person that they would come to know Jesus as their Lord and savior and be a great evangelist for God. I prayed that God would keep them from harm. Even after I prayed, I was pondering what does this mean. It was like the Holy Spirit said, So you like mysteries? Ok I have some mysteries for you--- spend time with Me, search the scriptures and uncover the mysteries I have hidden".

To pursue God's heart includes spending time with Him. He has so much to share with us. For me, wasting time is a barrier to pursuing the heart of God. This story while true is still unfolding because I am a work in progress. I desire to not be distracted by the cares of this world and therefore, I am asking God to give me grace and wisdom on not putting things before Him.

There are other barriers that may try to hinder our pursuit; they may be family or even financial barriers that try to still our thoughts and time away from God. There may be thoughts of not feeling worthy or not feeling equipped to begin and/or carry out the pursuit. No matter the barrier, decide today to ask God to bring forth deliverance regarding all barriers and strengthen you for the journey of pursuing Him.

Prayer

Father, I come before you with a heart full of reverence and appreciation. I thank You for guiding me and directing me. Father, in Jesus name, I ask that You forgive me of every sin of omission and commission. Lord renew my heart and give me a desire to seek You and serve you. Father Your Word instructs me to be vigilant in my pursuit of You and Your Kingdom. Your Word says:

Seek ye first the Kingdom of God and His righteousness and all these things will be added unto you (Matthew 6:33).

I am asking for grace to seek Your Kingdom and righteousness. I bind up every barrier that would attempt to come and prevent or delay my pursuit of You and Your Kingdom. Lord, I loose provision, grace, and mercy to be dedicated to the pursuit. I thank You for Your love and kindness towards me and that You have a desire to share with me Your mysteries. Speak to my heart Lord today and show me Your glory. In Jesus name I pray. Amen.

Day 13

Thought Exercise: In this section you reviewed a few types of barriers to pursuing God's heart. In the next three days you will think more deeply about barriers to pursuing the heart of God. Today, think about a barrier that you have that is hindering your pursuit of God's heart. It can be anything, anxiety, fear, disobedience, envy...etc. Search the scriptures and meditate on what God says about that barrier. Include the scriptures when you pray. Ask God to help you overcome that barrier.

Day 14

Thought Exercise: Not coming to God as a little child is a barrier to pursuing God's heart. This barrier is not spoken about enough. Jesus said:

"Assuredly, I say to you, unless you are converted and become as little children, you will by no means enter the kingdom of Heaven" (Matthew 18:3 NKJV).

Children are teachable, they know they do not know everything and expect to have a teacher. To pursue God's heart, we must be like little children at the teacher's feet receiving wisdom and knowledge. Meditate on *Matthew 18:3* today. Write out a prayer and ask God to reveal areas in your life where you are not or have not come to Him as a little child.

Day 15

Thought Exercise: To pursue God's heart, one must have a healthy reverence for God the Holy Spirit. Today read Acts Chapter 10. In Acts 10:19, the Word of God provides an example of obedience to the Holy Spirit. Ask God to speak to your heart and give you grace to obey the Holy Spirit. When we confess Jesus as our Lord and Savior, the person of the Holy Spirit comes to live inside of us. The Holy Spirit is the one who gives us power on Earth. The significant role the Holy Spirit plays in the lives of believers may be one reason Jesus strongly warns against blaspheming the Holy Spirit.

Also, I say to you, whoever confesses Me before men, him the Son of Man also will confess before the angels of God. But he who denies Me before men will be denied before the angels of God. And anyone who speaks a word against the Son of Man, it will be forgiven him; but to him who blasphemes against the Holy Spirit, it will not be forgiven (Luke 12:8-10).

Section 6: Missing the Heart of God

The issue with pursuing the heart of God is that sometimes we miss it. Sometimes we have every intention to seek God and behave in ways that please Him, but we fall short. Even in the natural, we put expectations on ourselves and then feel defeated if we do not reach those expectations.

When I was a student, I was a perfectionist. I worked hard, but I also struggled with depression if I did not complete tasks on time or if it took me too long to complete a task. I remember times when I was so defeated, I felt like giving up. Then one day the Holy Spirit spoke to me and said "Begin Again and Begin Today!

Journal Entry
12/22/2005

I hear the Lord saying: I want for you to seek out the very thing you think you know about. You are not accomplishing your goals because you are not pursuing Me as you should. Gather up all your possessions and pursue Me with everything you have. I am not a God of confusion. I do what I say I will do, but I need you to be obedient. Through faith you can move mountains but faith without works is dead. Holdfast to My unchanging hand and meditate on My Word. Delight yourself in Me and watch Me move on your behalf. I am a jealous God and I will not have anything before Me. To enter into the Kingdom I have for you, you must be obedient. It starts with your obedience and your diligence. You can do all things- Just Begin Again, and Begin Today. (Holy Spirit)

I listened and took those Words to heart. I understood that God wants partners to fulfill His will on Earth. Yes, I can stress and try to do things in my own power. Or I can trust and lean on Him for his direction and guidance. The decision to lean on Him is not a passive action. Leaning on God is active because sometimes He requires you to step out and do things that you would not normally do. I am writing this devotional as an act of faith and continue to lean on Him for His direction. I listened and am listening for His will. And I am here to encourage you to listen for the direction of the Holy Spirit. If there are areas in your life that you feel you may have missed God, do not dismay, just Begin Again and Begin Today. Begin again means to start over and do not allow the past experiences to deter you from reaching your goals. You have the ability to create a new start. Begin today- meant that I did not have to spend any more time wallowing in what did not happen, but I could step into today without the baggage from yesterday.

In other words, if you ever feel like you missed the heart of God, do not delay your new start. God wants you to know that you have not missed it. If you have breath in your body, you have an opportunity to get up and start over. He said Begin Again and Begin Today to free me from the bondage of distraction. Distraction is a tool that works to delay the fulfillment of assignments and purpose.

Just as we have times when we miss it in the natural, we also have times when we miss it regarding spiritual things and the things of God. But what we must remember is that God does not condemn us. When we decide to serve God, condemnation may try to come, but God is calling all fornicators, backsliders, robbers, gossipers...etc. It is true, these behaviors do not please God. He is a Holy God and desires for us to also walk in holiness, but while we have breath in our body God gives us opportunity to begin again. But we must take that opportunity and not delay in repenting and turning to Him (Begin today).

Yes, all have sinned and fallen short of the glory of God and it is only God's grace that can keep us on the path toward pursuing Him. But sometimes we unintentionally miss the heart of God. When God says that my people perish for the lack of knowledge (*Hosea 4:6*), He is saying that sometimes His children are in situations because of not having the necessary information to avoid or get out of those situations. Because God calls it a lack of knowledge that means that the knowledge is available to be known and His children just have not uncovered the knowledge.

Prayer

Lord, in Jesus name, I want you to know that I love you and adore You. Lord, I pray that you bring forth the necessary deliverance in my life. I know that deliverance is the children's bread (*Mark 7:27*). I confess my sins and repent. I understand that with repentance comes an actual change in behavior and mindset. When Jonah repented, He got up and got back on the path toward obedience (*Jonah 3:3*). Lord help me to be like Jonah. Help me to repent through both having a heart transformation and necessary action. Holy Spirit speak to my heart and guide me in the way that I should go. Forgive me for anytime I have missed the opportunity to please You. I pray that You give me wisdom. I know that it is Your will that I have an abundant life. I know that it pleases you to see me prosper. Bless me indeed oh Lord, enlarge my territory, and keep me from evil all the days of my life (1 Chronicles 4:10). In Jesus name I pray. Amen.

Day 16

Thought Exercise: Sometimes we intentionally miss God's heart. Yes, I said intentionally. I once heard Pastor Mike Murdock say that delayed obedience is disobedience. Pastor Murdock's message illustrated that there are two ways that someone can be disobedient to the will of God: 1) by not doing what God asks and 2) waiting to do what He has instructed.

When God told Jonah to go to Nineveh, Jonah decided not to obey the instructions. Meditate on *Jonah chapter 1* today. Think about areas in your life that you may be delayed in obeying. Pray and ask God to reveal to you areas of disobedience and to give you the grace to obey.

Day 17

Thought Exercise: Although at times we miss God's heart, we have an opportunity to begin again. Jonah did not stay in the fish's belly, but instead he made a conscious decision to obey God and obtained deliverance. When Jonah came to himself, he prayed to the Lord His God while he was still in the fish's belly. He did not wait for the fish to release him. He cried to God and it was that cry to God that helped Jonah get out of the situation.

When Jonah was released, and God gave Him the instruction to arise and go to Nineveh the second time, Jonah got up and went without delay. If you miss God's heart, be like Jonah and cry out to God in your situation. When He gives you directions, obey. Decide to Begin again and Begin today. Study the second instruction God gave Jonah. (Jonah Chapters 2 and 3). What happened when Jonah obeyed? Write out a prayer based on what you review today.

Day 18

Thought Exercise: Missing God's heart is also connected to giving up and allowing our circumstances to impact us to the point that we do not want to go forward. God intends for us to be victorious and has called us more than conquerors (Romans 8:37). Think about the story of the widow woman and Elijah. Most often this story is told from the perspective of Elijah! Where the widow woman obeyed the Word of the Lord given through Elijah. Usually, people do not discuss the level of "giving up" the widow woman was experiencing. Imagine what she was feeling when she was picking up sticks? She was distraught to the point that she was preparing to die (*1 Kings 17:7-16*)!

Take time today to read about the widow woman and consider areas in your life where you have given up. Then write a prayer and ask God to reignite you. He has started something good in you and He will complete it (*Philippians 1:6*).

Section 7: Be Intentional in Your Pursuit

Pursuing the heart of God is not something that can be done lackadaisically, one must be intentional. There are so many barriers and distractions that would try to come and prevent the pursuit of God's heart. The great news is when you are intentional about pursuing God, He is intentional about being found. I read the "Listening Prayer" by Dr. Mary Ruth Swope. This book is what I would call an oldy, but goody. It was published in 1987 but has so many insights and strategy regarding being intentional about praying and seeking God. In the book, Dr. Swope demonstrates the fact that prayer is not a one-way street. As she was intentional about listening in prayer and giving God an opportunity to speak to her, He spoke to her. Dr. Swope demonstrates that when we pursue God, we find God, but we must be intentional with our pursuit.

One of the first steps to being intentional when pursuing the heart of God is understanding that the condition of our heart matters to God. The Bible demonstrates that man looks at the outer appearance, but God looks at the heart (1 Samuel 16:7). There is something so mysterious and significant about the heart of man that God puts great emphasis on the heart.

Blessed are the pure in heart for they shall see God (Matthew 5:8 NKJV)

For where your treasure is, there your heart will be also. (Luke 12:34 NKJV).

The sacrifices of God are a broken spirit; A broken and a contrite heart, O God, You will not despise (Psalms 51:17)

He also reveres a heart that is faithful *(Nehemiah 9:8)*. The condition of man's heart is so important to God that He gives specific direction regarding how man should guard his heart and keep his/her heart set on God. The Lord promised to circumcise our hearts and the hearts of our descendants. He instructs us to love the LORD our God with all our heart and with all our soul, so that we may live *(Deuteronomy 30:6)*. God desires to circumcise our hearts, but also requires us to make a conscious decision to yield to Him and allow Him to work on our hearts. People of God set your heart toward God. A heart so set that you know what David meant when he said:

Seek My face," my heart said to You, "Your face, O LORD, I shall seek. (Psalm 27:8).

Prayer

In Jesus name, I proclaim-Father, You are so good to me. You have allowed me to take time to come to the knowledge of You. I know that You desire a one on one relationship with me. Forgive me Lord for any areas of sin in my life. Today God I ask for grace to pursue You. I ask for strategy, wisdom, and understanding as I pursue. Father, Your Word says:

"it is the glory of God to conceal a thing: but the honour of kings is to search out a matter" (Proverbs 25:2).

Father, as I chase after You, reveal Your plan. It is indeed my honor to have the opportunity to seek Your heart and Your Kingdom. Reveal to me Your mysteries. Give me the grace to obey the promptings of the Holy Spirit when You are calling me out to pray and spend time with You. Show me how to study to show myself approved (*2 Timothy 2:15*). Father I desire this new level of study not for my own glory, but for Your glory! I desire to know You intimately. I desire to honor You with my life. Lord help me to be intentional about the time I dedicate to pursuing after Your heart and after Your Kingdom. In Jesus name I pray. Amen.

For the next three days, there is a prayer to pray. After you pray the prayer, complete the exercise and watch God move on your behalf.

Day 19

Prayer: *Father, In Jesus name, I pray that you would bless me today. I choose to be intentional about pursuing Your heart. Give me what You would have me to pray. Thank You for hearing my prayers. You are a great God who does great things. I desire to learn of You. I desire to know You. Guide me today and I will be sure to give You all the praise, glory and honor. In Jesus name I pray. Amen.*

Thought Exercise: God's Word is a light unto your feet. Take His Word and write out a prayer that you can pray throughout the day regarding being intentional about pursuing His heart. You can use the scriptures that are provided or look in the Bible and find scriptures that fit the request on your heart.

Psalm 57:7-My heart is steadfast, O God, my heart is steadfast; I will sing, yes, I will sing praises!

Psalm 40:8-I delight to do Your will, O my God; Your Law is within my heart.

Psalm 9:1-I will give thanks to the LORD with all my heart; I will tell of all Your wonders.

2 Chronicles 17:6-He took great pride in the ways of the LORD and again removed the high places and the Asherim from Judah.

Psalm 119:11-Your Word I have treasured in my heart, That I may not sin against You.

Psalm 112:7-He will not fear evil tidings; His heart is steadfast, trusting in the LORD.

Psalm 119:10-With all my heart I have sought You; Do not let me wander from Your commandments.

Day 20

Prayer: In Jesus name, I proclaim-- You knew me in my mothers' womb and because You know the number of the hairs on my head, I know that You know me and my character. Father create in me a clean heart and renew a right spirit within me (Psalms 51:10). Cover me with the precious blood of Jesus. Father, I pray this day, that You would give me the grace I need to complete the desires that I have in serving You and seeking You. My head, hands, eyes, ears, mind, soul, all of me belong to You and I desire to seek You with my whole heart. Hear my heart Lord and let this prayer and request be pleasing unto You. Lord transform me from the inside out and have your way in my life. In Jesus name I pray. Amen.

Thought Exercise: Draw a picture of yourself. You do not have to be an expert artist. With your picture- pick out at least three body parts and write down how you plan to use those parts of your body to pursue the heart of God. Then open your Bible and identify scriptures that address the mind, body and soul. Use scriptures to write out a prayer regarding how you will use your mind, body and/or soul to pursue the heart of God.

Day 21

Prayer: In Jesus name, I proclaim that *only You, oh Lord, are my guide! In You I put my trust. I love You Lord. I desire after You. Whatever is in me or on me that is not pleasing to You, Lord, I am asking You to burn it up and cleanse me. God, as you revealed yourself to the children of Israel as the God of Abraham, Isaac, and Jacob. I pray that You do the same for me. You are the God that answers by fire (1 Kings 18). Give me direction and strategy on how to be intentional about pursuing after Your heart. I thank You right now because I know You have heard my prayer and are answering my request. Lord, I desire more of You. Show me Your heart and Your way and give me grace to honor You, reverence You, and live a life of Full Pursuit. In Jesus name I pray. Amen.*

Thought Exercise: Write out a plan for how you will be intentional about pursuing God's heart. What things do you have to let go of? What things must you start doing? Write out a prayer thanking God for showing you the plan and helping you to stay on the path He has for you.

Pursue God=Pursue Purpose

In 2005, the Lord said to me: "*In order for you to accomplish the plans I have for you, you must love to spend time with me, so I can direct your path*". But it was only until recently that I gained a deeper understanding of what God meant when He said the "accomplishment of His plan" required spending time with Him.

One day while I was driving, my daughter said, "Mom, why do people die?" That day, I talked to all of my children about reasons people die. Then I began to explain that everyone who is born will die, but before people are born God puts a plan on the inside of them. I taught my children that God sends people into the world to uncover His plan. To help them understand what I meant, I shared a short story.

I said, "Let me tell you about Ruth and Joshua. Ruth was born into the world with a God-given plan, but while she is in the world, she does not seek God. Even though she has accepted Christ as her Lord and Savior, she seeks after her own heart's desire and never takes the time to ask God what He desires for her life. When she dies, she leaves the Earth and goes to Heaven, but she does not accomplish the plan God had for her.

Now Joshua was also born into the world with a God-given plan. During his life, Joshua faces challenges but makes conscious efforts to seek God, pray, and pursue after the things that are pleasing to God. Joshua chooses to honor God with his life. While he is on the Earth, he comes to understand that he is man and God is God. He understands that he is part of a bigger picture and there is something God has given him to do on Earth. During Joshua's life, he pursues God's heart and His will. Joshua learns about the plan God has for his life and partners with God to accomplish the plan. God opens doors for Joshua to walk out the plan.

God gave Ruth and Joshua a purpose and a planned destiny, but Joshua is the only one who uncovered God's plan (the purpose for his life). Ruth did not pursue God's heart and when she died, she did not complete the purpose for her life. When Joshua died, he left the Earth having accomplished the plan that God had for him.

This Ruth and Joshua story helped my children understand that God is the one who has given them a purpose and they must seek God to accomplish His plan. The story also helped me to understand that the biggest difference between Ruth and Joshua is not connected to salvation or God loving one more than He loves the other. The difference between Ruth and Joshua was their pursuit of God. When Joshua made up in his mind that he was going to partner with God, he positioned himself to be about God's business.

It does not matter if you are 5 years old or 85 years old. You can ask God to fulfill the purpose for your life. Today, ask God to fulfill the purpose for your life. Tell Him that you want Him to have His way in your life. Tell Him you want to be about advancing His Kingdom agenda. And then be prepared to relinquish emotions that would try to get in the way of you attaining the great purpose that God has for you.

Recently, my mother-in-love, encouraged me to watch Bishop TD Jakes' message on "Hemotions". I love and honor her, so I obeyed her guidance. After watching, I completely understood the revelation that Bishop Jakes is giving to the world. In the message, he talks about how men respond to the cares of this world and how they handle stress. "Hemotions" is a great message describing how women must be able to support their men (sons, brothers, husbands) during "turns" in life. I am in full support of the message.

When I finished watching the video, I thought to myself, "Wow men experience so much, but those Hemotions are subject to deliverance. For deliverance is the children's bread (Matthew 15:26)"! The truth is we are in a battle and the enemy would want us to stay focused on how we are dealing with our emotions. When God is saying, **"Grab ahold of the authority that I have already given you and beat back emotions, mindsets, behaviors and anything else that would try to hinder the assignment I have given you to do on this Earth. It is time to awake"**.

And *do* this, knowing the time, that **now *it is* high time to awake out of sleep; for now, our salvation *is* nearer than when we *first* believed. The night is far spent, the day is at hand.** Therefore, let us cast off the works of darkness, and let us put on the armor of light. Let us walk properly, as in the day, not in revelry and drunkenness, not in lewdness and lust, not in strife and envy. But put on the Lord Jesus Christ, and make no provision for the flesh, to *fulfill its* lusts (Romans 13:11-14).

Men of God must get the necessary deliverance and get on post to be available and useful in this spiritual battle. Jesus is coming back and when He comes, He is looking for a bride that is on assignment! Our position is to pray for deliverance from these Hemotions. We must ask God to put Godmotions in place of Hemotions. It is a new day! I am not saying Hemotions are not real, I am saying God desires for us to not live out of emotions. I believe focusing on emotions is a trick of the enemy. Did Jesus have Hemotions? No, he had Godmotions. He surrendered His emotions and focused on being about His Father's business. We have to come to the place that we are focused like Jesus. We must lay down emotions to pick up our assignment. We must be like Jesus and spend time with God to gain strength to accomplish the call God has on our lives. We must work the works of Him who sent us while it is day (John 9:4).

Both Hemotions and Shemotions need deliverance. It is time for the Body of Christ to study and pursue deliverance, so we can be free to do the work God has commissioned us to do. I am not an expert in deliverance, but the ministry gifts Apostle John Eckhardt and Apostle Ivory Hopkins are well-versed in the matter.

What I do know is everyone must get to the place of praying that the Holy Ghost fire burns up anything that is not like God. The Body of Christ must die to self (our flesh). We cannot continue to walk around as though it is business as usual! We cannot operate from the old way of doing things. God is a right now God and He is doing a right now thing. We must get in line and on our post; shake ourselves loose and get in the battle! We must relinquish the cares of this world that cultivate distractions and take the time to hear what God is saying right now! The time is now! There is an urgency in the spirit for the church to wake up! **Children of God awake in Jesus name.**

This awakening is for the Body of Christ as a whole. No matter where you feel you are in your relationship with God, there is opportunity to go to another level. It does not matter where you are (in church, not attending church or never been to church). It is not even important who you are (whether you are an ordained minister or not). God is interested in you leveling up in the spirit. I recently attended a prayer conference hosted by Apostle

Stephen Garner. When I left that conference, God was showing me that I needed to go to the next level in prayer. There is always another level in God that we can attain if we have a desire to pursue Him and obey His direction.

God is love and He desires for us to pursue Him, but the pursuit is a choice. He gives us freewill and we either obey or disobey His direction. God leaves place for grace because He truly desires us, but the truth is our God who is Love also gets to the place where He rejects people because of their disobedience.

Then the Spirit of God came upon Zechariah the son of Jehoiada the priest, who stood above the people, and said to them, "Thus says God: 'Why do you transgress the commandments of the LORD, so that you cannot prosper? Because you have forsaken the LORD, He also has forsaken you.' (2 Chronicles 24:20)

When we pursue God's heart, we align ourselves with what pleases God. This pursuit helps us to stay focused and to avoid mindsets and behaviors that would cause us to forsake God. When we pursue God's heart, we are equipped to put forth actions that please God, where God does not feel forsaken. Remember God is a relational God. A relationship with God is just like any other relationship in the natural. For instance, you know what things please your best friend, so you work to do the things that please them. Also, you know the things that displeases your spouse, so you work to avoid doing the things that displease them. You care about building relationship with your friends and family, so you endeavor to please them. If you choose to not put forth effort to please your loved ones, know that you are operating from a place of self-centeredness and selfishness where what pleases you is put above what pleases those you love.

This concept is the same when we think about pleasing God. When we put things before God and we do what displeases Him, we put our desires above God's desires. It is difficult to build relationship with God when we do not consider the things that please Him. He tells us to seek first His Kingdom because He knows when we seek His Kingdom we are seeking after His heart. He knows that when we pursue His heart, we align ourselves to fulfill His purpose for our lives, and when we align ourselves to fulfill purpose, we are choosing to serve Him. So, the question is will we (the Body of Christ) pursue or not pursue God, for He desires our service.

"Blessed is the Lord God of Israel, For He has visited and redeemed His people, And has raised up a horn of salvation for us in the house of His servant David, As He spoke by the mouth of His holy prophets, who have been since the world began, That we should be saved from our enemies And from the hand of all who hate us, To perform the mercy promised to our fathers

and to remember His holy covenant, The oath which He swore to our father Abraham: To grant us that we, being delivered from the hand of our enemies, might serve Him without fear, In holiness and righteousness before Him all the days of our life (Luke 1:68-71).

Conclusion

The heart is important to God. He desires for our hearts to be aligned with His, and the only way this alignment occurs is by pursuing His heart. To be in Full Pursuit of God's heart, we must come to God as a little child with humility. If you confess to love God, then pray and pursue His heart. If you desire a closer relationship with God, you are in good company because God desires a closer relationship with you. The Lord is waiting for His children to grab ahold of the revival He is sending. At a recent spiritual gifts workshop, my pastor, Apostle Andrew Bell, was teaching a wonderful message about God's children tapping into the realm called obedience. Apostle Bell said, "Those who love God obey God". After hearing this Word, I wondered how people can fully obey God if they do not know His heart. There are some who believe they know the heart of God yet walk in unforgiveness or even operate under the guidance of hate. We (God's children) must have a desire to truly know God's heart.

All throughout the New Testament, Jesus can be found healing the sick, raising the dead, and teaching about the Kingdom of God. Jesus was and is on assignment to do what He knows is the will of God the Father. On Earth, Jesus was about the Father's business and Jesus fulfilled His purpose because He sought God the Father. He was intentional about obeying the will of God. Like Jesus we can accomplish our God-given purpose through seeking and obeying God. The Bible says:

"Thou shall love the Lord God with all thy heart, and with all thy soul and with all thy strength, and with all thy mind; and thy neighbor as thyself" (Luke 10:27 NKJV).

I believe that Jesus operated from this "new testament commandment". He loved God with all his heart. He loved God so much that to accomplish God's plan He gave the ultimate sacrifice. He gave His life so that we could truly live. Jesus loved God with His soul. The soul is the will, mind, and emotions of a person. Jesus loved God with His soul through keeping his heart focused on the will of God. Jesus' mission was to do the will of the Father.

Now I think it is very telling that God saw fit to instruct us to love God with our minds two times in Luke 10:27. Even though the mind is a part of the soul, God chose to be very clear and repeat the instruction for us to-love Him with our minds. This focused instruction tells me that the mind is a place where we will have to be doubly diligent at focusing on God and what He desires. I believe that the mind is likened onto a command center and all the other areas (heart, will, emotions, strength) are rooted in the thought processes of the mind. Joyce Meyers once said where ever the mind goes the man follows.

Well, I agree with that statement. Wherever the mind goes the heart, will, and emotions follows.

The mind also directs the level of strength one has. It is in the mind that we either believe or do not believe in ourselves, our worth, and our ability. The mind holds the key to one's pursuit of purpose. For instance, if in your mind you do not believe that you are worthy of love or capable of doing great things for God, then you would not have strength to do great things. However, if in your mind you have confidence in the One who called you, and you know that you cannot do anything apart from God, then you would seek God to get the strength you need to do the impossible. Loving God with all your strength is about knowing He is the one who gives you your ability, and then seeking Him to receive the power to do what He desires.

It is in the mind that we choose to love our neighbors as ourselves. In fact, in our mind we define who are neighbors are. Some feel that their neighbors are only their family members and close friends and anyone outside this circle of people does not deserve to be loved by them. Other people may feel that their neighbors are only those who are of the same race/ethnicity or religion as them, and everyone else does not deserve their love. It is in the mind where a person decides that their neighbors are those who God desires for Himself. This person believes that if God desires no one to be lost (2 Peter 3:9), then their neighbor is mankind (everyone). People who believe their neighbor is mankind do not operate from a place of racism, sexism, hate, or division. They love their neighbor (mankind) as they love themselves, doing good to all, especially to those who are believers in Christ Jesus.

Therefore, as we have opportunity, let us do good to all, especially to those who are of the household of faith (Galatians 6:10 NKJV)

We (the Body of Christ) are of the human race and our focus must be about seeking first the Kingdom of God. Jesus gave clear direction that we (the Body of Christ) are to seek first the Kingdom of God.

Seek ye first the kingdom of God and His righteousness and all these things will be added unto You (Matthew 6:33).

Because the mind is so important, we must be diligent in keeping our minds and thoughts clean and pure. When we pursue God's heart and seek first the Kingdom of God. We focus on what is important to God and we allow the Holy Spirit to cleanse us of anything that is not like God.

The truth is that everyone who believes they are serving God may not be obeying the heart of God.

*Not everyone who says to Me, 'Lord, Lord,'
shall enter the kingdom of Heaven, but he who does the
will of My Father in Heaven. Many will say to Me in
that day, 'Lord, Lord, have we not prophesied in Your
name, cast out demons in Your name, and done many
wonders in Your name?' And then I will declare to
them, 'I never knew you; depart from Me, you who
practice lawlessness! (Matthew 7:21-23 NKJV)*

As God's children we must come to the place
where we say, "**Lord Not Our Will, But Your Will
Be Done**". We must come to a position of pursuit
where His will being done and obeying His
promptings is the most important thing. Self is set
aside and putting God first is our focus. The truth is
that God is love and if we are living in and/or
operating in systems where love is not resonating, we
should know there is a problem. The love God has for
mankind continues to echo throughout generations
as God gave His only begotten son for mankind.
God's expectation is that we would love Him, love
ourselves, and love others. The only way we can
truly operate out of love is through having a renewed
mind and a tender heart. The mind and heart are
transformed as we pursue God's heart by getting into
His Word and spending time in his presence.

The church is a "Sleeping Giant" and God
desires to bring about a great awakening. He is
requiring that we put first things first and pursue
after Him. When we pursue after Him, we are

positioned to be Ephesian 4 Believers. I will share more about what God has shown me about being an Ephesian 4 Believer in a subsequent book, but what you need to know is when you pursue after God you will arrive at purpose.

When God created you, He created you with a purpose. God never intended for you to live without Him. In fact, He acknowledged in His Word that "I [God] am the vine you are the branches if you abide in me [God] you will produce much fruit," (John 15:5). God clearly has shown that pursuing after Him is connected to pursuing after our capacity to fulfill purpose.

God is a God who desires relationship with His children. Seek Him and He will be found of you (Jeremiah 29:13). Seek to know God the Father, God the Son and God the Holy Spirit and you will be positioning yourself to know who you are, and how you can accomplish all that He created for you to accomplish.

Just as Smith Wigglesworth is considered a General of Faith, and Apostle Ivory Hopkins is a General of Deliverance. I consider Myles Munroe to be a General of Purpose. He taught that the wealthiest place is the cemetery. He said that we should work and pray that we die empty. "Dying empty" means that whatever God has placed on the inside of you is birthed before you transition from Earth to Heaven! Pursuing after God's heart is the first step to accomplishing your God-given plan and fulfilling purpose. Pursuing God's heart is not just about you, but also about those connected to you. What you learn in your pursuit will help your children, family, loved ones and all those in your sphere of influence.

Make up your mind to be intentional about your lifelong pursuit of God! Do what you can do and let God do the rest! Continue your journey with great expectation in God, the One who desires your pursuit. He has so much to share with you. Prophet Daniel Pringle is a prophet who frequently ministers at my church. In his book, "Prayers that Bring Results" he tells of how he signed up for the School of the Holy Spirit. Be like Prophet Pringle and enroll in the School of the Holy Spirit. Allow the Holy Spirit to guide you and instruct you on your journey through life. Although this devotional is coming to an end, do not lose momentum. Continue in Full Pursuit of God the Father, God the Son, and God the Holy Spirit.

It is important for the Body of Christ to pursue God's heart and reverence the persons of the Holy Trinity. Yes, we must love, honor and reverence God the Father and God the Son, but we cannot leave out God the Holy Spirit. Even Jesus proclaimed that the Spirt of the Lord God was upon Him and He was anointed to preach good tidings to the meek and do great things.

The Spirit of the Lord God is upon me; because the Lord hath anointed me to preach good tidings unto the meek; he hath sent me to bind up the brokenhearted, to proclaim liberty to the captives, and the opening of the prison to them that are bound; To proclaim the acceptable year of the Lord, and the day of vengeance of our God; to comfort all that mourn; To appoint unto them that mourn in Zion, to give unto them beauty for ashes, the oil of joy for mourning, the garment of praise for the spirit of heaviness; that they might be called trees of righteousness, the planting of the Lord, that he might be glorified (Isaiah 61:1-3).

The Holy Spirit gave Jesus power and it is through the power of the Holy Spirit that we will do the greater works that Jesus said we would do. Jesus said:

Verily, verily, I say unto you, He that believeth on me, the works that I do shall he do also; and greater works than these shall he do; because I go unto my Father (John 14:12).

There are greater works that God intends the Body of Christ to accomplish. These greater works will be done through the power of the Holy Spirit. Evangelist David Diga Hernandez has a message on Encounter TV (YouTube) entitled "We need the Holy Spirit". In this message Evangelist Hernandez eloquently describes the importance of the Holy

Spirit in helping us fulfill the plan of God. Find some time to listen to this message.

Body of Christ, the Holy Spirit is a gentleman. He is not going to force us to welcome Him in to our lives. We have to choose to be yielded vessels. We must decide that we are willing to do what is required to usher in God's Kingdom agenda.

Make a conscious decision to partner with the Holy Spirit. Partnering with the Holy Spirit is about surrendering your will and focusing on God's will. It is by the Holy Spirit that you are able to accomplish the plans God has for you. When you partner with the Holy Spirit you become a yielded vessel for God's service.

Please know that you are important to the Body of Christ. In fact, you play a vital role in God's Kingdom plan. Continue to take the time to pursue God and be focused on fulfilling the plan God has for your life.

Appendix

Confessing Jesus as Lord and Savior

If you have never confessed Jesus as your Lord and Savior, repeat the following prayer and believe in your heart that God hears you.

"Heavenly Father, I come to You in the Name of Jesus. Your Word says, "Whosoever shall call on the name of the Lord shall be saved" (Acts 2:21). I am calling on You. I pray and ask Jesus to come into my heart and be Lord over my life according to Romans 10:9-10: "If thou shalt confess with thy mouth the Lord Jesus, and shalt believe in thine heart that God has raised him from the dead, thou shalt be saved. For with the heart man believeth unto righteousness; and with the mouth confession is made unto salvation." I do that now. I confess that Jesus is Lord, and I believe in my heart that God raised Him from the dead."

(Salvation; Kenneth Copeland Ministries)

Today, submit your will to Jesus. Go tell someone that you have given Jesus your life. You are ready to enter the realm of Full Pursuit (see page 27). Continue to seek God and ask Him to direct your path.

Re-dedicating Your Life

If you have previously been saved by grace but want to re-dedicate your life to Jesus, repeat this prayer and you will be renewed from the inside out.

Heavenly Father, in the name that is above every name, Jesus, I come with my hands and heart lifted. I choose You and the plan you have for my life. Forgive me for every area of sin. I remind you of your Word. You said: "if My people who are called by My name will humble themselves, and pray and seek My face, and turn from their wicked ways, then I will hear from heaven, and will forgive their sin and heal their land" (2 Chronicles 7:14 NKJV). Well Lord, I repent and am humbling myself before you. I pray that you continue to guide me on this journey of pursuing You. Today, I turn from everything that is not like you. Hear from heaven, forgive my sins and heal my land and everything connected to me. Jesus, I know that You are Lord and you are risen from the dead. Now revive my heart and re-ignite me to fulfill your Kingdom agenda. I decree and declare; I am operating from the realm of Full Pursuit. In Jesus' name I pray. Amen.

Baptism of the Holy Spirit

Are you filled with the Holy Spirit with evidence of speaking in tongues? God desires to fill you to overflow with Himself. Pray and tell God that you desire the manifestation of the Holy Spirit in your life.

In Jesus name, I come to You with great expectation. For I know that I am saved by grace through faith and that not of myself. I understand that salvation and being your child is a gift you have given me (Ephesians 2:8). Lord you are so generous, you even delight to give me the Kingdom (Luke 12:32). I receive the Kingdom that you are so pleased to give me, and I also ask to be filled with the Holy Spirit with evidence of speaking in tongues. Your Word says: "if ye then, being evil, know how to give good gifts unto your children: how much more shall your heavenly Father give the Holy Spirit to them that ask Him?" (Luke 11:13). Father, I want you to know that I agree with your desire to give me the Holy Spirit. Fill me up to overflow. Holy Spirit speak through me (Acts 2:4) and let your power move through me (Acts 1:8). Lord have your way and I will forever praise Your Holy name. In Jesus' name I pray. Amen.

Dedication

Father God, thank you for your faithfulness in allowing me to share the Word you have given me for your people. I pray that this Word falls on good ground. I pray that you prepare the hearts of the people so that they are ready to fully enact the direction you have provided. Father let me and those who read this devotional be like Jesus. Let us do what we see You doing. Let us be like King David, people after Your heart. I pray that everyone who reads this devotional will find purpose through pursuing you. They will pray for their purpose to be fulfilled and will be intentional about partnering with you to accomplish your Kingdom agenda. Let their heart cry be to see your Kingdom come on Earth as it is in Heaven. To those who are learning of you, give them a desire to enlist in the Army of the Lord. And to those who know you, give them strength to put on their full armor from the top of their head (helmet of salvation) to the soles of their feet (gospel of peace) and fight the good fight of faith. For it is a good fight because with faith in You, we win. Lord on behalf of the heirs of salvation everywhere, I pray- **Lord Not Our Will, But Your Will Be Done**. I bind up anything and everything that would attempt to delay, detour or cancel the assignment that you have for your children. I bind, rebuke and cast down any backlash, retaliation, and transfer of spirits. I loose your peace, joy, protection and provision upon your children. I plead the blood of Jesus upon all those you desire for yourself. In the mighty name of Jesus, I pray. Amen.

Dr. Roland Wesley, you were more than a social worker with a PhD. You were more than an entrepreneur. You were more than an advocate for education. You were more than an Alpha Phi Alpha fraternity man. You were even more than a visionary. You were an amazing father and grandfather. You will forever be a great role model for me and everyone else you encountered while you walked this Earth. You taught me to work hard and to care for those in the community. You took me to church and introduced me to God the Father, God the Son, and God the Holy Spirit. I am so thankful that God saw fit to give me a portion of your passion for empowering individuals, families, and communities. I pray that as you look down from Heaven, you are pleased with my efforts to change the world by positively impacting those in my sphere of influence.

Anthony Osei, you are my father, and I want you to know that you are always in my heart and on my mind. I pray that God constantly provides you an open heaven. I pray that as you continue to delight yourself in God, all of your dreams come true.

Companion Journals

Made in the USA
Lexington, KY
12 May 2019